SCIENCE ENCYCLOPEDIA

ECOLOGY

An imprint of Om Books International

Contents

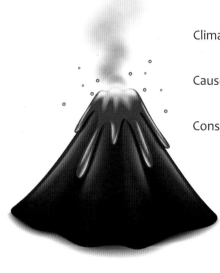

ECOLOGY

The word ecology was coined by German zoologist Ernst Haeckel, who applied the term ökologie to the "relation of the animal both to its organic as well as its inorganic environment". The word comes from the Greek word oikos, meaning "household", "home" or "place to live". Thus, ecology deals with the organism and its environment. The concept of environment includes both the organisms themselves and their physical surroundings. It involves the relationships between the individuals within a population and between the individuals of different populations. These interactions between the individuals, populations, and organisms and their environment form the ecological systems or ecosystems. Ecology can thus be defined as the study of the relationships that exist between all living things and their environment. Scientists who study ecology are called ecologists.

Biosphere

In the term biosphere, bio means life and sphere means surrounding. Scientists use the term sphere for describing various parts of Earth where life exists, such as atmosphere, lithosphere, hydrosphere, geosphere, anthrosphere and cryosphere. All these spheres, together, constitute the biosphere. The layer of gases around Earth is called atmosphere. Lithosphere is the solid surface layer of Earth and hydrosphere is the layer of water that makes our planet look blue.

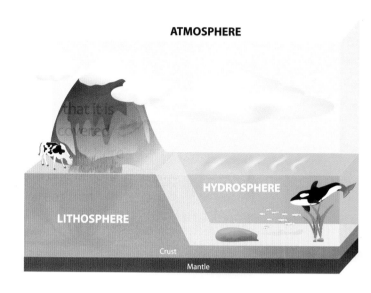

The hierarchy of biological organisation as can be seen in our biosphere.

What is the extent of the biosphere?

Biosphere is the global-ecological system, which is the home of all living organisms along with their surrounding environment. From the depth of the oceans to the highest mountains, every place where life is possible comes under the biosphere. Even the microorganisms that we find deep underground and the birds that fly very high and look like a dot to us, come under the biosphere. After so much progress in science, it is still not possible to define the boundaries of our biosphere.

Effect of non-living factors on living organisms and vice versa

The evolution of life can be studied from non-living matter itself. That is why they remain correlated to a great extent, influencing each other. All the living organisms on Earth are very closely related to their surroundings; they get adapted to their surroundings for their survival. As many natural factors affect our life, like rotation, revolution and the tilt of Earth's axis, even minuscule changes in the weather and air can change our climate. Biologically and chemically, too, Earth undergoes change continuously.

Biodiversity

In 1968, American biologist Raymond F. Dasmann gave the term, biodiversity to the world. Biodiversity or biological diversity is the variation in the life found on Earth along with all the natural processes. Biodiversity includes variations in a gene, ecosystem and species.

Why is it important?

You would have heard or read somewhere that tigers are in danger and the number of tigers is decreasing very fast. The government is taking steps to save this species. Do you know why these measures are important? What will happen if there are no tigers left? Being the carnivorous and dangerous animals that they are, you might want to get rid of them, but they should not disappear as every species is important for life on Earth.

As we know, there is a great bonding between living organisms and their surrounding environment; they both depend on each other. By the destruction of any species, the food chain gets disturbed. This affects the ecosystems and, simultaneously, the life of human beings as well.

Distribution of species

We cannot find the same type and number of species everywhere. They are unequally distributed, depending on various factors like altitude, temperature, type of soil, physical features and the other species found in the area. The highest biodiversity is found in the areas of rainforests.

Human, the main culprit

During the early life of human beings, the number of species living on Earth was very large. But as human beings made progress, the number of species decreased steeply. Because of human beings, there have been great changes in climate, seasons, atmospheric gases, water and land. These changes, in turn, affect the habitats and behaviours of different species, and cause their extinction.

SILENCE PLEASE !

RESPECT THE ORANGUTANS

Hydrologic Cycle

Our Earth is known as the "blue planet". Do you know why? Because three-fourth of the planet is covered by water. But we cannot see so much water around us as its distribution is not uniform. We also cannot find all of the water in liquid state.

What is the water cycle?

You know how on heating, water evaporates and changes into water vapour. Similarly, when you keep ice outside the freezer, it melts quickly into water. So water goes from one state to another with the change of temperature. This occurs in nature too. Here, water continuously moves from one state to another and from one resource to another.

The journey of water, when it circulates from land to sky and back again, is called the water cycle or hydrologic cycle. The water cycle can explain the existence and movement of water on Earth.

Water moves through all four areas of Earth: atmosphere, lithosphere, hydrosphere and biosphere. In this process, it is stored in the atmosphere, oceans, lakes, rivers, soils, glaciers, snowfields and groundwater.

The whole cycle involves various steps and interactions with the physical processes in this journey.

Role of the water cycle

As you would have heard, the human population is growing at a very fast pace. Just think how much water each individual consumes in a day and how much of it goes down the drains.

Water cycle is the process that circulates water throughout the globe, and makes it clean and available to us. Rain water is known to be the purest of all forms of water on Earth.

Water cycle is always related to the transfer of energy, so it is responsible for temperature changes.

There are many other roles played by the water cycle, like sedimentation and erosion, which help in shaping geological features.

Many ecosystems depend on the water cycle for their existence. The flow of water and ice transports many materials across the world.

A symbolic representation of how pollution in cities is affecting ice at the poles.

Percolation

Even plants sweat (transpire) just the way people sweat (perspire). Transpiration is the process by which plants lose water out of their leaves. It gives evaporation a tiny hand in getting water vapour back up into the air.

Global water distribution

Over 96 per cent of our world's total water supply is saline. Furthermore, of the total freshwater, over 68 per cent is in the form of ice and glaciers. Another 30 per cent of freshwater is present in the ground. Thus, fresh surface-water sources, such as rivers and lakes only comprise approximately 1/150th of one per cent of the total water.

This is why it becomes necessary for us to save water. The rate at which we are using water is very high as compared to the rate at which the water cycle takes place. Hence, it becomes important that we use water very carefully and save as much of it as possible, every day.

A visual representation of how water travels through our environment to create the life encouraging water cycle.

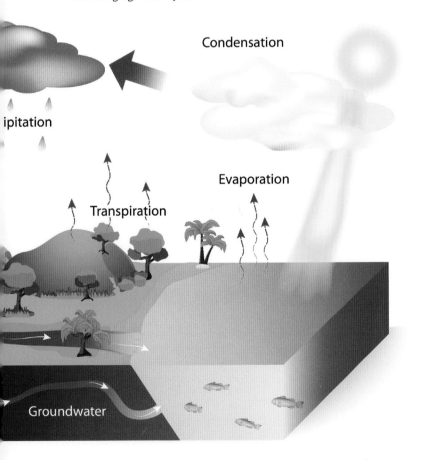

Condensation

ipitation

Evaporation

Transpiration

Groundwater

Various processes of water cycle

Evaporation

The Sun, which is the source of heat and light, drives the process of the water cycle. Water from resources like seas, lakes, oceans and land gets evaporated by absorbing heat. Evaporation is the process of conversion of water into water vapour. Plants also lose water by the process of transpiration, which keeps them cool. This is like plants sweating. This water vapour in the atmosphere moves, but is not visible to us. Water vapour, due to its low density as compared to other gases, reaches a great height.

Condensation

This is the process by which the clouds that we see in the sky are formed. As the water vapour rises up, it encounters low temperature, and condenses into water droplets, forming clouds.

Precipitation

Air currents move the clouds from one place to another, making them collide, fuse, grow and fall out on Earth's surface as precipitation, as they become too heavy for the air to keep hold of. In cooler regions, water falls down as snow and we enjoy snowfall.

Collection

The rainwater then either goes into the oceans, rivers or it may fall on land. When it falls on land it increases the levels of groundwater, which is used by plants, animals and human beings for drinking and many other purposes. Some of the water goes deep underground to form aquifers. Aquifers hold fresh water for a very long period of time.

Runoffs

Water moves across the land as runoffs. These include both surface and channel runoffs. Water also evaporates back to the atmosphere or can be extracted for human consumption.

Ecosystem

In the rainy season, you would have seen many plants growing around your home. For your study, take any one that has not been disturbed for many days and observe the different types of organisms and insects in it. There are some non-living factors that support their growth, like sunlight, water, temperature, pressure, nutrients and turbulence in the place. This plant is a simple example of an ecosystem.

Definition

Ecosystem is the term used for the community of living organisms that live, stay, feed, reproduce and interact in the same area or environment. An ecosystem is always accompanied by the energy flow and cycling of elements between the biotic and abiotic components present in it. An ecosystem can be as small as a plant and as large as a desert or ocean.

An ecosystem can be described as the study of the flow of energy and materials through organisms and their environment.

Classification

There are different types of ecosystems as climate varies from place to place. Broadly, ecosystems are classified into two categories: the aquatic ecosystem and terrestrial ecosystem.

Aquatic ecosystem includes marine and freshwater ecosystems while terrestrial ecosystem largely depends upon the type of dominant vegetation. It is further divided into categories like forest, littoral, riparian, urban and desert. The term biome is used for the vegetation types, such as tropical rain forest, grassland and tundra.

Each component is essential

Do you understand why everything is interconnected? To understand, perform a small test. If you obstruct the sunlight reaching the plant that you observed, all living organisms will diminish slowly as every plant depends on sunlight and each organism feeding on the plant depends on them for their life. Thus, each and every part of an ecosystem works together in a balanced system.

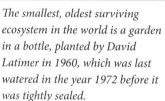

FUN FACT

The smallest, oldest surviving ecosystem in the world is a garden in a bottle, planted by David Latimer in 1960, which was last watered in the year 1972 before it was tightly sealed.

Oxygen

Water

Light energy

Carbon dioxide

Minerals

Process of photosynthesis by which plants convert sunlight into energy.

What is the process of ecosystem?

While studying an ecosystem, attention is mainly focussed on the functional aspects of the system. The functional aspects include the amount of energy produced by the process of photosynthesis, that is, by a biotic component and how this energy flows through other organisms via the food chain.
The whole process can be understood as energy enters the biological system in the form of light energy and changes into organic molecules via photosynthesis and respiration, and is further converted into heat energy that is used by organisms for various activities.

The nutrients also continuously get recycled in an ecosystem. It goes from one organism to another and also gets decomposed. Elements, such as carbon, nitrogen and phosphorus enter the life cycle and, sooner or later, due to excretion and decomposition, get mixed with abiotic components, completing the cycle.

Threat to ecosystems

An ecosystem can be considered healthy if each and every species living in it is not being damaged by human interaction, natural disasters or climatic changes. Fire, storms, floods and volcanic eruptions are some of the natural disasters faced by various ecosystems. An ecosystem can be regarded as healthy and sustainable when all the elements are in balance, and all the species reproduce and contribute in increasing the biodiversity.

Littoral

Forest

Fresh water

Aquatic Ecosystem

Terrestrial Ecosystem

Ecosystem

Marine

Riparian

Urban and desert

An image representing the objects that smoke affects.

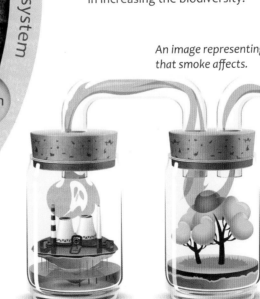

Marine Ecosystem

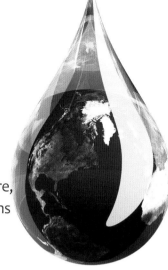

We know that there is over 70 per cent water on Earth's surface. Therefore, the marine ecosystem is the largest ecosystem in the whole planet. Oceans and seas constitute 97 per cent of the total water content.

A horseshoe crab lives in a salt marsh.

What is a marine ecosystem?

Though we have five main oceans, the marine ecosystem can further be divided into many smaller ecosystems depending on the types of species found in them. These include salt marshes, intertidal estuaries, lagoons, mangroves, coral reefs, deep sea, sea floor, rocky shores, submarine canyons, seamounts, chemosynthetic ecosystems, open slopes, deep basins and many more.

Why study it?

Scientists are continuously studying the ecosystems in order to preserve them, as every ecosystem has its own special role to play for existence of life on Earth. A marine ecosystem is different from a freshwater ecosystem due to its high salt content.

The marine ecosystem is very important as it affects terrestrial climate greatly. Wind circulation, rainy season, weather of coastal regions and current production are all under the control of the oceans' movements.

Life at sea

Presently, one million species of the ocean are identified, but scientists say that there are approximately nine million species that still need to be identified and classified.

In response to the various conditions available in the ocean, different types of animals and plants live here. It includes many plants, such as the phytoplanktons and algae like kelp. Many fishes like shark, swordfish, clown fish, eel and seahorse are found here. Among the mammals living in the sea are blue whales, walruses and otters. Octopus, cuttlefish, oysters, snail and slugs are the types of molluscs living in the ocean.

Organisms living in the ocean can also be classified, depending upon their eating habits, as producer, herbivorous, carnivorous and scavengers.

Ocean light zones

When we peep into a well or a deep tank, we can barely see anything. Imagine shining a light on the water surface. There will still be complete darkness at the deepest bottom of the tank and no light can reach it. Similarly, the deep areas in oceans are much deeper than the height of Mount Everest at some places. The ocean is divided into three zones based on the amount of light that penetrates it. Sunlit or euphotic zone is the uppermost layer of the sea or ocean where light can shine through and 90 per cent of the organisms exist here.

Twilight or disphotic zone is the middle zone getting extremely minuscule light. Organisms producing their own light by bioluminescence exist here.

Midnight or aphotic zone is the deepest part of the ocean. In this zone, it is always too cold and dark, just like a freezer, but it can be lit. Only a few animals can live here, mainly those who can survive by getting energy from the cracks.

Maximum light penetrates to the uppermost layer of the sea.

Man and sea biome

A large biodiversity is found in the marine ecosystem and it is considered as having great resistance towards invasive species and other changes that cause the depletion of various species. However, human beings are causing disturbance in the marine ecosystem. Some fishing practices like bottom trawling, disposal of oil and other wastes, over fishing, growing demand for seafood and coastal developments are all causing damage to this sea biome.

FUN FACT

The Great Barrier Reef off the coast of Queensland, Australia, is the world's largest coral reef. It is made up of 2100 individual reefs and 800 fringing reefs, and is the only living organism that's visible from space.

11

Aquatic Ecosystem

Aquatic ecosystem is the ecosystem that is present in the water bodies on our planet. There are complex and intricate interactions between organisms and their environment. All organisms live, feed, reproduce and exchange matter and energy inside water bodies. The water may be fully saline, brackish or fresh. Marine habitats range from coasts and continent shelves to the deep sea. A great biodiversity is found because of variations in temperature, pressure, salinity, wind, wave action, tides, currents, light and substrate.

The coral reef is an example of a marine ecosystem.

Fresh water ecosystem.

Types of aquatic ecosystem

Aquatic ecosystem is classified into two categories: freshwater ecosystem and marine ecosystem. These two types of ecosystems are extremely diverse in structure. The physical constraints and opportunities are quite separated. Of the 70 per cent water on our planet, only one per cent of water constitutes fresh water and most of it is frozen in the polar ice caps.

In the marine ecosystem, sodium, chlorine and other dissolved materials constitute 85 per cent of the total composition. Life is believed to have evolved in saltwater as many phyla of animals live here.

Freshwater ecosystems are also very diverse in nature. Lakes, ponds, rivers, streams and wetlands with a good range of depth and flow rates come under this category. They are classified under lentic, lotic and wetlands. Of the world's known fish species, 41 per cent are found in the freshwater ecosystem.

A place where the river meets the ocean is called an estuary; it is usually shallow and very productive in nature.

View of an estuary.

Life in water

Animals like planktons, crayfish, snails, worms, frogs, turtles, insects and fishes are found in the freshwater ecosystem. Plants found in this region are water lilies, duckweed, cattail, bulrush, stoneware and bladderwort. Its biome varies dramatically from small trickling streams to wide rivers.

About 80 per cent of the solar energy reaching the ocean is absorbed in the first 10 m. Most deep-sea organisms are nourished by organic matter fixed by photosynthesis near the surface. There are entire biological communities on the seafloor that are nourished by chemosynthesis on the ocean floor and not by photosynthesis at the surface.

The Hawaiian green sea turtle of the aquatic ecosystem.

FUN FACT

The deep ocean displays the blue colour of pure water often called a "biological desert" as the open ocean is an area nearly devoid of life.

Importance

The aquatic ecosystem is very important for life on Earth. Can you imagine how our lives depend on aquatic organisms? Just take into account how often you need water from the time that you wake up till the time that you go to bed every day. If we use water so extensively, from where will we get pure water for drinking? Though we have studied that Earth is 70 per cent water, not all water is fit for drinking. Therefore, it is a limited resource, which is purified by aquatic organisms.

Let's get back to the fact that the aquatic ecosystem purifies water, recharges ground water and recycles nutrients that are used by human beings. Moreover, they can attenuate floods. Freshwater ecosystems are a good source of water for human beings as the water is used for many purposes like drinking, producing electricity and transportation.

A major portion of oxygen demanded by the human population is met by algae and other plants of the oceans.

The largest electric power producing facility in the USA is the Grand Coulee Dam on the Columbia River (freshwater ecosystem).

Freshwater Ecosystem

The term "freshwater" itself clarifies the condition of the water being fresh, having less salinity and good for consumption. Lakes, ponds, rivers, streams, springs, estuaries and wetlands are included in the freshwater ecosystem. From the total of 70 per cent water on Earth, only one per cent is available as fresh water and another two per cent is in a frozen state on the polar caps.

Comparison of biodiversity

Biodiversity is more when the depth of the ocean is less.

Biodiversity in oceans depends upon light and nutrients from the coastland. As we go deeper and farther from the coast, the biodiversity will go on decreasing. However, in case of lakes and ponds, as they are comparatively smaller and shallower than oceans, light can penetrate deeper. In winter, due to their stagnant water, they often freeze, creating an anaerobic condition inside the water.

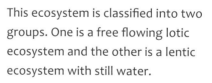

Classification

This ecosystem is classified into two groups. One is a free flowing lotic ecosystem and the other is a lentic ecosystem with still water.

Ponds and lakes come under the lentic category. The temperature of lakes changes over time. Based on the type of biotic community, four zones are found in lakes. These are littoral, limnetic, euphotic and benthic.

Streams and rivers constitute the lotic ecosystem. Light, temperature, flow and chemistry are factors affecting the biome in this ecosystem in which water is more oxygenated due to the flow.

Waterfall is a free flowing lotic ecosystem.

FUN FACT

Do you know which is the largest freshwater lake (in terms of volume) on Earth? It is Lake Baikal in central Asia.

Freshwater biome

Depending upon the size of the ecosystem, the number of organisms differ but the basic structure remains the same.

As we know, the base of any food chain in any ecosystem is occupied by the plants producing food by photosynthesis. In a freshwater ecosystem, different types of plants, mosses and algae are found. In flowing water, they have a special capacity to attach to the place instead of being carried away. In sources where water is stagnant, water lilies, algae and duckweed can be seen in floating state.

A variety of fishes, birds, insects, amphibians and crustaceans are found here. In estuaries, many clams, shrimps and fishes are found.

A turtle in still water.

Role of freshwater ecosystems

Freshwater ecosystems act as natural filters, reducing pollution, controlling floods and providing food and habitat for aquatic organisms. They are very important for energy production, transportation and recreation.

We get water for drinking from freshwater resources only. Of the total fish species that we enjoy in our food, 40 per cent exist within freshwater itself.

Threats on freshwater ecosystem

As human beings work progressively daily for making their life easier and safer, they are neglecting the conservation of the ecosystem. As ecosystems are very essential for each organism's survival, we should strive to preserve them.

Overuse, dams, pollution, diversion and non-native species are among the threats faced by freshwater ecosystems. Acidification, eutrophication and pesticide contamination are the major chemical stresses faced by them. Also, global warming is the cause of floods and drought faced by all organisms and human beings.

The global extinction rate of freshwater species is four to six times higher than the marine or terrestrial ecosystems.

How can we prevent this from happening to the ecosystem? Each and every individual can take some steps for preserving this. We love to visit clean parks with many fishes and birds near it and it is possible to observe them only by keeping them clean and by conserving water.

Forest Ecosystem

What comes to your mind when you come across the word "forest"? You tend to form a picture in your mind of different wild animals, birds and insects living in a dense cluster of trees. Thirty eight per cent of Earth's surface is covered with these forests. In different types of climates, forests with different variety of flora and fauna are present.

Definition

"Forest ecosystem" is the term used for biotic and abiotic components and their interactions with each other, and with the environment in the forest.

Informally, we can say that different species of animals, birds, insects, microorganisms, trees, herbs and shrubs living together and exchanging energy is called a forest. Abiotic components include the surrounding air, climate, soil, water, organic wastes, rocks, pebbles and so on.

Types of forest ecosystems

Though forest ecosystems are too diverse to study, they are classified into three groups based on their location on Earth.

1. **Rainforests**

    The forests found in the tropic region near the equator are rainforests.

2. **Temperate forests**

    These are located between the regions of taiga and the rainforests. Because of their location, these forests have a moderate temperature and four distinct seasons occur here. The soil of these forests is very fertile because of a good amount of rain.

3. **Taiga**

    These are located in the northern hemisphere.

Biodiversity

Adaptation is the main phenomena to determine which type of species can be found in a particular ecosystem. For example, we can find pine and fir trees in the colder regions but not in the hotter regions. Different types of adaptations, such as shape and size of the leaves, depth of the root and fur or hair on the body of the organisms are found.

Thus, by knowing the climatic conditions, we can assume which type of species will be able to survive in a particular ecosystem. Furthermore, the complexity of the forest will indicate the biodiversity found in it.

Types of flora and fauna

To understand the biodiversity found in forests, it is necessary to divide the forest into layers.

Canopy

The topmost layer is the layer of tall trees called the "canopy". These trees provide shade to the entire forest, filtering sunlight, other radiations and rain. In this way, they protect the lower layer of trees and organisms. They also have deep roots so that they can face challenges from the environment like wind, storm, lightning and meet their water requirements.

The animals found in this layer are birds, tree frogs, snakes, lizards and hard-bodied insects.

The Understory

This is the layer of the forest that has trees, which are not yet fully grown or haven't reached their maximum height. The layer of canopy not only protects them from direct sunlight and rain, but also causes them to grow at a slower rate.

Because of their thinner foliage, the biodiversity of animals found here is quite great. Birds, butterflies, caterpillars, frogs and tree mammals like varieties of squirrels, raccoons and monkeys are found here.

The shrub layer

This is the layer of forest covered by shrubs, which are short woody plants. Different types of spiders, insects, birds, snakes and lizards live here.

The olive shrub.

Forest floor

The floor of the forest where mosses and a variety of flowers grow always remains covered with humus, making it more fertile. Hornets, butterflies, birds, worms, slugs, snails, centipedes, millipedes and many microorganisms get nourished here.

A wide range of vertebrates, non-vertebrates and microorganisms are found in the land of forests, which continue the food chain.

Role of forest ecosystem

The forest ecosystem plays a vital role for the survival of life on Earth. It cleans the air, regulates the water cycle, prevents drought and flood, gives wood and many other food products, prevents air and noise pollution, regulates the cycle of nitrogen, magnesium, phosphorus and calcium, and makes the soil fertile.

FUN FACT

The boreal forest, or the sub-polar taiga, is a vast tract of unbroken forests found in the northern hemisphere between the tundra and the taiga. These forests of evergreens are frozen for almost nine months in a year.

Trees protected by the canopy come under the understory.

The tallest tree is the canopy.

17

Desert Ecosystem

If we ever visit a desert, we would be surprised to know that it is also a type of ecosystem. One-fifth of Earth's surface is covered by deserts. Although the number of plants and animals living here is quite low, it is still a vital biome to study. More than one billion people live on the land of the desert. These are the areas that receive less than 10 inches of rain per year.

Deserts are extremely cold during the nights and extremely hot during the days.

Definition

"To desert" means "to abandon". The deserts are the arid, dry regions on Earth having animals, plants and microorganisms adapted to these harsh conditions.

At least one desert is present on each of the continents except Europe and Antarctica. The Sahara desert in northern Africa is the largest desert on Earth.

Types of deserts

We mostly know of deserts which are hot and dry, but some cold deserts also exist on Earth. These are the deserts of Antarctica and Greenland, where vegetation is very rare, like in the hot deserts.

FUN FACT

The Sahara Desert, the longest desert in the world, is located in northern Africa, spanning across 12 different countries.

Components of ecosystem

Organisms can remain alive in this harsh and dry environment with adaptations only. These areas don't receive rains frequently and when it rains, organisms adapt to make use of these infrequent short periods of great abundant rainfall.

Abiotic components include latitude, longitude, soil and climate.

Biotic components comprise these classifications:

Producers

Plants like cacti, creosote bush, sagebrush, rice grass and salt bush are found in deserts. These have adaptations as follows:

1. They can store and find water with roots scattered at a shallow level to absorb little rainfall.
2. They have broad leaves with a waxy coating.
3. Thorns and deadly poisons are present on the body of the plant.

Consumers

Locusts, yucca, darkling beetles, ants and arachnids are some insects living in deserts. Among reptiles, rattle snakes, lizards and frilled lizards are adapted to this life. Gila woodpeckers, roadrunners and galahs are among the birds living here. Some mammals like hamsters, rats, kangaroos, horses, foxes and lions live in this ecosystem. Camel, the ship of the desert, is the most important mammal found in this ecosystem.

Decomposers

Some bacteria and fungi are found here.

Cactus is an example of a producer.

Camels are the consumers.

Role of the desert ecosystem

They are brilliant locations to farm solar energy. You would have witnessed a lot of windmills in these areas. They play a role in tourism and recreation. Unlike other ecosystems, human beings are not depleting desert land, but increasing them.

Primary characteristics of the deserts

Low rainfall and more evaporation are the main features of deserts. These are clear lands and we can see for miles with the naked eye.

The Sun shines brightly during the day, causing sand to warm up to a 100 °C at some places with very low humidity. The exact opposite is true for the nights.

Clouds don't visit these deserts. Can you imagine a sky without clouds? Clouds form a covering or a blanket which can decrease the amount of the sun rays entering Earth's surface. As there are no clouds, no water bodies and not even vegetation that can absorb the heat, the days become too hot and the nights become too cold.

The soil is very dry and low in organic nutrients but rich in minerals. Not all deserts have only sand; some have rocks, pebbles or red sand mixed with it.

Man saving himself from the scorching heat of the desert.

Problems Faced by Earth

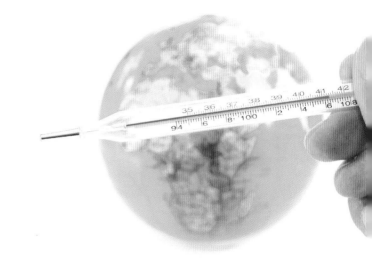

Whenever we want to take a beautiful picture, we stand near a beautiful flower or a flowering plant. We feel relaxed when we are on a nature walk. We try to maintain a garden in our house.

Why does everyone love to be in the lap of nature instead of being in a concrete building? It is because Earth is really the mother of life. The different ecosystems living in it have their own beauty. However, we have currently distanced ourselves from nature and, as a result, nature too has turned its back on us.

Earth Day

A graphical representation of our future if we continue polluting the environment.

What are the problems faced by Earth?

On 22nd April, we celebrate Earth day. Why is there a need to celebrate this day? It is to alert and educate people regarding the necessity of conserving nature and taking up the habit of recycling waste materials.

There are enormous problems that Mother Earth is facing today. Among them, the major problems are extinction of species, global water crisis, global warming, energy or oil consumption, deforestation, desertation, air pollution, overflowing landfills, mining, population explosion, ocean currents, erosion, climate change, clearing land for agriculture, introduction of invasive species and many more.

What should we do?

Recycling of materials, preserving water, conserving power and planting trees are some of the ways by which everyone can contribute to saving our Earth.

FUN FACT

The UN Intergovernmental Panel on Climate Change (IPCC) is established for fighting climate change problems.

Issues Earth faces

Some of the major problems that have blown up to monstrous proportions are:

1. Population explosion

Our present growth rate is over 75,000,000 people per year. In the near future, there will be a rising need for everything: house, food, clothes, jobs, etc. For meeting the demands of an increasing population, we will have to clear more lands for agriculture, dig more mines, establish more industries, clear more forests and use more chemicals for increasing the productivity of agriculture and industries. We will use a higher amount of natural resources and pollute the environment more. Scientists are assuming that after a few centuries, if the population explosion is not controlled, we will end up striving for our basic needs.

Overpopulation

2. Pollution

Human beings are consuming and polluting too much. There are different types of pollution: air, water, noise and soil pollution. We are progressing at a fast rate but we must also take into consideration the implications that it has on our environment. What will happen if the air we breathe is not pure or the water we drink is not safe?

All natural resources are limited. The main problem is how we access them, our manner and efficiency.

We are polluting the atmosphere by eliminating our gaseous wastes in it. This is responsible for the rise in temperature across the globe and global warming. We are diminishing and polluting our own freshwater resources as well by releasing our wastes, chemicals, etc., in them.

Heavy smoke from industries leads to polluted air.

3. Global warming

Our pollution has created a hole in the ozone layer, whose job is to protect us from harmful radiations of the Sun. We have damaged our protective layer, because of which we are facing many skin problems, cancer, etc. It is also affecting plants and animals.

4. Climate change

In May 2015, Nepal faced a massive earthquake, causing a lot of casualties. In 2010, China saw floods and a heat wave struck Russia. The reason is that our planet is getting warmer day by day. We are releasing gases like carbon dioxide in the atmosphere, which are responsible for this warming. We are facing hot summers, cold winters and rains in any season of the year. This is only the beginning of climatic repercussions.

Global warming and climate change leads to melting glaciers that in turn affects the habitat of the living organisms that balance the Earth.

5. Mining

We dig Earth to obtain iron, copper, nickel, diamond, granite, etc. As a result of mining, we are disturbing ecosystems by releasing poisonous wastes in water, cutting plants and destroying the habitats of animals.

Mining destroys land and soil, and imbalances the ecosystem.

Water Pollution

Water pollution is the contamination of water bodies like rivers, lakes and ponds by chemicals, radioactive substances, pathogens, microbes, etc., causing modifications in the physical, chemical and biological properties of water. The main cause of water pollution is dumping untreated wastes in the rivers and lakes. It is difficult to imagine it but if you throw even a single empty bottle of sunscreen or plastic bag into the river, you become a contributor in the increasing water pollution.

Causes of water pollution

For an ideal society, clean and plentiful water is a necessity, but our activities and development are constantly hurting this natural resource. The major causes of water pollution are:

1. Sewage waste
This includes human wastes from paper to plastic and whatever we flush out into septic tanks. In some places, these are linked to the water sources and are polluting them. Sometimes, during rain, the sewer line overflows and pollutes waterbodies.

2. Agricultural waste
Fertilisers, pesticides and insecticides used by farmers can get into water through runoff. Animal waste pollutes lakes and streams when it gets washed away into them.

3. Industrial waste
Industrial waste drains into rivers introducing lead, cadmium, mercury and polychlorinated biphenyls in it. Poisonous gases released in the air mix with the rain and reach waterbodies.

4. Radioactive waste
Nuclear power plants, industries, medical and scientific centres release radioactive waste into water and have long-lasting effects on humans.

5. Plastic
Plastic is used in our daily life. It is non-toxic and non-degradable, and remains in water for hundreds of years. It harms fishes and affects the ecosystem.

Measures of controlling pollution

Awareness – People should be made aware of water pollution, its effects and control measures.

Wastewater treatment plants – More treatment plants with greater filtering capacities should be established to properly treat water.

The laws – The government should enforce strict laws for controlling pollution.

Check runoff – Runoffs from mines and quarries should be regularly checked to prevent them from connecting to water sources.

By applying some practices at an individual level, for example, by using environment friendly products, reducing the use of pesticides and insecticides, knowing what to throw in the drains and toilet pots, we can control water pollution.

Polluted Yamuna river near Taj Mahal in Agra, India.

Air Pollution

Air pollution is the contamination of air, which changes the physical, chemical and biological characteristics of the atmosphere. It affects all other ecosystems on Earth. Industrial chimneys, people smoking in public places, cars running without pollution check are some factors causing air pollution.

Main sources of air pollution

Coal was the source of air pollution in olden days but is rarely used now. Some sources of pollution are:

1. **Fossil fuel burning** – About 96 per cent of sulphur dioxide is released in the atmosphere by burning coal and petroleum products, and from power plants and industries. Vehicles release carbon monoxide and nitrogen oxides into the air, which we end up breathing. Even traditional biomass plants cause pollution.

2. **Ammonia** – Today, to enhance productivity, a lot of fertilisers, pesticides and insecticides are used in agriculture that release ammonia in the atmosphere. Ammonia is the most hazardous gas found in the atmosphere.

3. **Industries** – Many pollutants like carbon monoxide, hydrocarbons, organic compounds and harmful chemicals are released by different manufacturing industries and petroleum refineries.

4. **Mining** – Most of the workers and people living in the areas near mining places suffer from many respiratory diseases because of harmful gases, dust and dirt.

5. **Household** – Main household pollutants are particulate matter, new paint, cooking smoke and tobacco fumes formed by smoking.

Effects of air pollution

Do you know about the great London Smog that occurred in 1952? It was the result of air pollution covering the whole city with a blanket of smog with no air to breathe and no visibility.

Global warming, introduction of greenhouse gases in the atmosphere and a hole in the ozone layer are the major effects of air pollution.

Acid rain is also a monster generated from air pollution. It can have an adverse impact on all living organisms coming in its contact.

Pollution also affects wildlife in their migration and adaptations. It also causes eutrophication in water sources.

Air pollution causes mortality rates to increase significantly. It causes respiratory infections, heart diseases, chronic obstructive pulmonary disease like emphysema and chronic bronchitis, strokes, lung cancer, asthma and also affects the central nervous system.

Children are more susceptible to respiratory diseases because of the presence of soft tissues in their respiratory organs.

What can be done to control air pollution?

Some steps can be useful towards controlling air pollution individually. These are the use of public transport, conserving energy, developing a habit of recycling, using energy efficient devices, etc.

Although the government has taken steps and formulated laws for controlling air pollution, it should be made stricter to make people obey them. The Clean Air Act is also a step towards creating and maintaining a healthy community.

Pollution over a city.

23

Other Types of Pollution

Pollution is the contamination of the natural environment with foreign substances or naturally occurring contaminants. Pollution affects the whole ecosystem: the air we breathe, the water we drink or the land on which we build our homes.

We are familiar with a few types of pollution, such as air and water pollution. Let's look at the different types of pollution that have different causes and consequences.

Oil spill near the beach.

Artificial lights have various side effects.

Types of pollution

Some forms of pollution that Earth is facing are:

Soil pollution

If we visit a construction site of any house or a place where the land is burrowed deeply, we will observe that the soil there contains a lot of plastic materials, some polythene bags and a lot of garbage. This condition is termed as soil pollution.

It happens because people litter without thinking how it would affect the environment. If we throw an empty packet or bottle or litter on the roadside, then we, too, are contributing to soil pollution.

Household dumping and littering, sewage spills, oil spills, radiation spills, industrial wastes and extensive use of chemicals in agriculture, like pesticides, insecticides and fertilisers, to increase productivity are some of the sources of soil pollution. Mining of different substances completely changes the soil quality in that area and affects the ecosystem gravely.

Soil erosion, shortage of food, water pollution and desertification are some of the consequences of soil pollution.

Light pollution

When we excessively use artificial lights on the roads, highways and at home all night, it is termed as light pollution. It affects the sleep cycle and is responsible for hormonal changes in the bodies of organisms.

Noise pollution

People generally use loudspeakers when they are celebrating or have a personal occasion. Even on the road, we can hear a lot of horns and other loud sounds.

NOISE POLLUTION

All these noises not only affect the hearing ability of human beings but also of the animals living nearby. If a newborn is exposed to such loud sounds, there is a high possibility that it may have an adverse effect on its delicate ears.

You would be surprised to know that the presence of trees can absorb most of the sound. This can be one more reason to encourage tree plantation.

Thermal pollution

Around the world, the summers are becoming hotter as compared to a decade ago. This is because we are making Earth hotter and hotter, day by day due to our activities.

Thermal pollution occurs when excess heat is released into the air or water during any process and has long-term effects. Many of the power plants and industries use cold water from lakes and rivers to lower the temperature of the plant parts. This water is then released back to the lakes and rivers. This activity kills many fishes and plants living there, disturbing the whole ecosystem.

There are many more reasons for thermal pollution, like building of more cemented floors and releasing heat trapping particulates in the air. Also, the trees and water sources which can absorb heat are diminishing very rapidly from the scenario.

Radioactive pollution

It is a rare type of pollution but extremely deadly as well. It occurs due to accidents of nuclear power plants or leakages. Improper disposal of the radioactive wastes is also one of the reasons behind this pollution.

The severity of this type of pollution can be estimated by considering the case of World War II, when USA attacked Hiroshima and Nagasaki with nuclear bombs, killing millions of people and infecting those who were left alive, along with their future generations, with deadly diseases.

Measures for controlling pollution

Pollution, in all its types, has an adverse effect on the environment. Thus, it is necessary to take steps for its control. Many countries worldwide have encouraged their legislations for the enforcement of laws to control such types of pollution.

But as good citizens, we too can help in this initiative by some practices like recycling, reusing, waste minimisation, checking our vehicles regularly for pollution, not littering anywhere, etc. Thus, we are the ones who can make our Earth clean and green.

Recording heat generated at the chimney with infrared thermal cameras.

Nuclear bomb attacks had severe side effects on cities.

FUN FACT

Delhi in India is the most polluted city on the planet in terms of air pollution.

Approximately, 80 per cent of waste in India is dumped in the river Ganga.

River Ganga in Varanasi.

Population Explosion

Population explosion is a major obstacle in the progress of any developing country. The term "population explosion" is used to indicate the rapid growth rate of human beings in a short period in an area. This gives rise to many other problems like shortage of food, place, jobs and every natural resource on Earth.

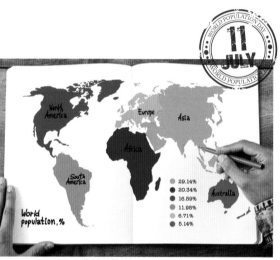

A colour coded map of the world denoting the densely and the sparsely populated continents.

The population density of Sao Paulo, Brazil is 9000 people per sq km.

World population explosion

According to the records, in 2013, the total world population was 7.2 billion. It has jumped drastically in a few hundred years. It is the estimation of the United Nation Population Fund that the population of the world would be around 10 billion by 2025.

The approximate ratio of three births over one death is found in countries worldwide. Among them, the more developed countries have effective population control as compared to less developed countries.

Consequences of population explosion

1. Increase in different types of pollution
2. Unemployment
3. Lack of proper food and nutrition
4. Poverty
5. Housing problem
6. Lack of proper education facilities
7. Faster depletion of natural resources
8. Increase in competition in every step of life of an individual

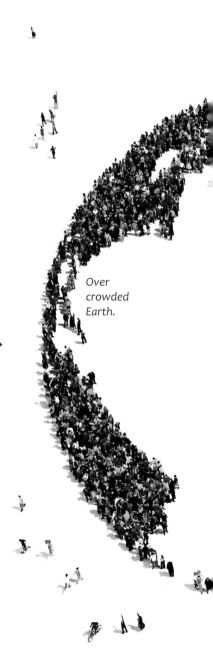

Over crowded Earth.

Reasons of population explosion

There is a progressive advancement in the field of science, daily. We are stressing more on hygiene, sanitation, nutrition and proper growth requirements. All these factors increase the birth rate and decrease the death rate, giving a longer life to human beings. This is the reason for overpopulation.

Birth rate

Previously, people would plan bigger families because most children died before reaching the age of 5 or 6. When the industrial revolution happened, there was an unbelievable advancement in the fields of science and technology, and many medicines, vaccines and treatments were discovered, which increased the survival rate of the infants.

Poverty

It is also one of the reasons for the increasing birth rate. People produce more children for having more earning hands in the family. Also, people under the poverty line have no means to get contraception.

Cultural norms

Backward thinking people keep believing in their cultural belief and prefer a boy child to a girl child, and as a result, keep conceiving till a boy is born, increasing the size of their family.

In some religions, abortions are frowned upon while others are against contraception. People who have blind faith refuse to use contraception in spite of it being available.

Death rate

Overpopulation can affect the economic growth of a country very seriously. But, it cannot stop advancement in the field of science. Humans have won over many deadly diseases and discovered various treatments. This has decreased the death rate from 12.5 in 1981 to 8.7 in 1999.

Immigration

Immigration decreases the chances of job opportunities and education in developed countries. Progress in the fields of transport, industries and agriculture has played an important role in overpopulation too.

Controlling measures

There are many birth control measures available in the market, and the government is making them popular and inspiring people to use them. As it is not possible to increase the death rate, we can only control the birth rate.

Adopting will also help in the education of impoverished children rather than adding to the population.

Immigration

Climate Change

We see that from time to time, it rains even when it is not monsoon. This change in seasonal pattern is very strange and is the result of disturbance in the whole ecosystem of Earth. This term is called climate change.

What is climate? What are the factors affecting climate?

Climate is the weather condition of a place, which stays the same for a long period of time. It doesn't stay the same forever and also changes from place to place. It depends on various factors like the amount of sunlight received by Earth, proximity to oceans and altitude, plate tectonics, volcanic eruptions and biotic processes. If the factors influencing climate are imbalanced, it will result in a change of climate.

Extremely hot summers are an example of climate change. Most countries reach a temperature of 46 °C or above. The reason can be that either too much heat is entering Earth or not enough amount of heat is going out. As climate change is a global problem, we need a remedy that can be implemented at a global level.

Climate change can be caused by either "internal" or "external" mechanisms. Whether the mechanism is internal or external, the resulting response of the climate system might be fast, slow or a combination.

Over 100 people participated in the global warming attention march in New York City.

FUN FACT

The amount of carbon dioxide being released into the atmosphere today is the highest than it has ever been in the last 650,000 years!

Earth is turning into a fireball

Sun is the primary source of heat for Earth. Radiations emitted from the Sun are absorbed by Earth's land, oceans and plants, and this makes the planet hotter. The amount of radiations absorbed by Earth always vary depending upon its position relative to the Sun. During the night, the light absorbed is radiated back to space. The land can radiate more heat as compared to water sources and vegetation. This is the reason why deserts are colder at night.

In the lower atmosphere, there is a layer of gases like carbon dioxide, methane and nitrous oxide, which together constitute the greenhouse gases. These gases have the capacity of holding heat. Thus, they prevent Earth from becoming a ball of frozen ice at night. This is the natural phenomenon for maintaining a moderate temperature through the day and night, making survival of life possible on Earth. However, current changes in the system have altered this mechanism.

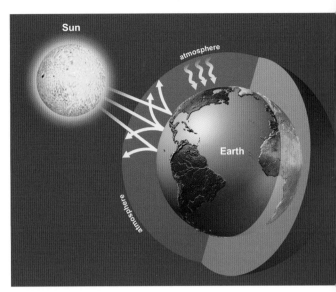

The greenhouse effect.

Disturbance of the natural phenomena

We are increasing the quantity of greenhouse gases to a very high level. We are burning fossil fuels, such as coal, petroleum products and oil, cutting down trees and clearing land. This is all increasing carbon content in the atmosphere.

If we observe, from 1900 to present date, the atmospheric concentration of carbon dioxide has increased from 300 ppm to 400 ppm (part per million). The carbon content level has increased to the extent that our planet has become engulfed in a thick, heat-trapping blanket.

Our planet is becoming warmer day by day. Over the past century, the average global temperature has gone up by almost 1 °C, which is also known as global warming.

Effect of high temperature on the habitat of living organisms in polar regions.

Adverse results of climate change

This high temperature of Earth is melting glaciers and increasing sea levels, chances and severity of storms, floods, wildfires and heat waves.

Earth's average temperature is expected to rise by as much as 4 °C over the next.

Causes of Climate Change

Climate is the long-term weather condition of a place. Climate change is the change in temperature, precipitation, winds and other factors for a prolonged time. Although climate has been dynamic since millions of years, it has come under scrutiny since the last few years. This is due to the speed of climate change and its effect on human beings and other species.

Climate change affecting the world

Scientists are continuously studying the reasons for climate change to find solutions for it.

Scientists of NASA have even researched whether we should blame the Sun for this climate change or not. However, they found that we should not, because the Sun plays no role in this climate change.

Global warming is a change that occurred much faster than any other climate change. Since the late nineteenth century, global temperature has gone up by 0.85 °C.

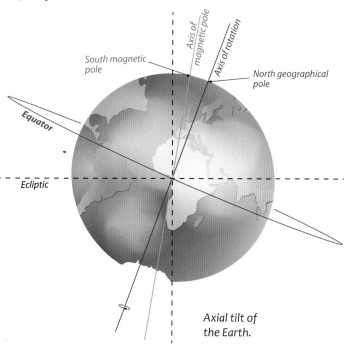

Axial tilt of the Earth.

Causes of climate change

Continental drift – Scientists have collected fossils of plants and animals from various continents and have discovered that approximately 200 million

Before   **After**

years ago, all continents were a part of a large land mass. Subsequently, they got separated and moved apart forming different continents with variations in climates. Scientists believe that this drift has not stopped and continues to take place even today.

Volcanoes –
Though volcanic activities are episodic, studies have shown that the large volume of gases released by volcanic eruptions can stay for long in the atmosphere and influence the climate.

Earth's tilt –
Earth's tilt is responsible for the various seasons of land. An increase in the tilt will lead to an increase in the severity of the season. As we know, Earth revolves around the Sun in an orbit. Its axis of revolution is not fixed, but there is always some gradual change in the direction of the axis. This change in axis can be a reason for climate change.

Consequences of Climate Change

Have you noticed the extremely high temperatures that we are facing these summers? This is happening in almost all the countries. Scientists have declared that by around 2050, many species will lose their lives because of this rise in temperature. In the twentieth century, we are facing a 17.2 °C rise in temperature. It has caused serious changes in the environment that will affect our lives in the long run.

Consequences

Human beings have brought about permanent alterations to our planet's geological, biological and ecological systems.

Type of weather
Every weather we experience is becoming more extreme. We are experiencing more hot days and fewer cold days. Some tropical regions receive extreme precipitation. The frequency, length and intensity of heat waves striking the surface of Earth have greatly increased. Increased temperature means increased evaporation of water; this acts as a fuel for storms and hurricanes. Chances of flooding, wildfires and drought conditions have gone up.

Cryosphere
The cryosphere is the part of land that is permanently covered with snow and ice. There have been observations that the ice on the Arctic sea has decreased greatly, alpine glaciers are melting and the ice cover of the Northern parts is greatly reducing. This molten ice, upon mixing in oceans, makes them hotter.

Increase in sea level.

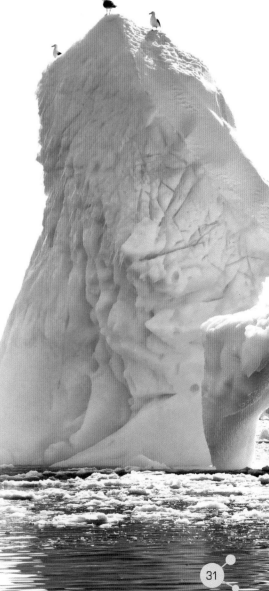

FUN FACT

The occurrence of climate change-related incidents have increased four fold between 1980 and 2010.

Oceans

Carbon dioxide, the gas that is most responsible for climatic change, is absorbed in large quantities by oceans. It causes the acidification of ocean water. Approximately 90 per cent of the heat released in the atmosphere is absorbed by oceans, which makes them hotter and causes them to expand.

Food supply and food security

A major concern is to find new sources of food, in case of uncertain rainfalls or fluctuating weather conditions. Farmers also face unexpected attacks of weeds, diseases and pests. This is the reason that the cost of the food grains is increasing day by day. Transportation is also affected by hot weather and flooding that causes scarcity of many commodities.

Soil cracked with weed that resulted in barren land.

Health

Smog is greatly increased because of hot climatic conditions. It causes the spread of asthma among other health issues. Many diseases like cancer are spreading because of the harmful rays of the Sun. The extension of wildfires causes the degradation of the quality of air. Fresh water is affected by the rise in temperature supporting the production of different pathogens. Health is greatly influenced by climatic change because of the decreasing quality of food, air and water. The agriculture industry and economy have also been affected.

Water resources

Water resources have been affected to a great extent. Many aquatic species have reached the edge of extinction due to climatic changes. Flood and droughts are common and also affect the forest ecosystem.

Dead fish due to floods.

Migration and conflict

In the future, there will be a conflict for the basic needs and tendency of all living organisms, including human beings, to migrate in search of a better place. The coasts will be wetter, the mid-continental areas will be drier and the sea level will rise unexpectedly.

Species extinction

There are many ecosystems that are at a risk of collapsing due to the change in weather. Coral reefs in the oceans, which are sensitive towards small changes, are deteriorating. As ice melts on the Polar regions, animals like polar bears and walruses are starving for food. The number of endangered species is increasing day by day.

Wild animals migrating for better living conditions.